**W9-ASL-402**

## DATE DUE

| | | | |
|---|---|---|---|
| | | | |
| | | | |
| | | | |
| | | | |
| | | | |
| | | | |
| | | | |
| | | | |
| | | | |
| | | | |
| | | | |
| | | | |

# Land Battles
## of the
# Revolutionary War

**Diane Smolinski**

**Series Consultant:
Lieutenant Colonel G.A. LoFaro**

Heinemann Library
Chicago, Illinois

© 2002 Reed Educational & Professional Publishing
Published by Heinemann Library,
an imprint of Reed Educational & Professional
Publishing, Chicago, IL

Customer Service  888-454-2279

Visit our website at www.heinemannlibrary.com

Designed by Herman Adler Design
Printed in Hong Kong

06 05 04 03 02
10 9 8 7 6 5 4 3 2 1

**Library of Congress Cataloging-in-Publication Data**

Smolinski, Diane, 1950-
    Land battles of the Revolutionary War / Diane Smolinski.
        p. cm. -- (Americans at war. The Revolutionary War)
Includes bibliographical references and index.
    ISBN 1-58810-274-2 (lib. bdg.)
    ISBN 1-58810-560-1 (pbk. bdg.)
    1. United States--History--Revolution, 1775-1783--
Campaigns--Juvenile literature. [1. United States--
History--Revolution, 1775-1783--Campaigns.] I. Title.
II. Series: Smolinski, Diane, 1950-      .
    Americans at war. Revolutionary War.
    E230.S66 2001
    973.3'3--dc21
                                    2001001618

**Acknowledgments**
The author and publishers are grateful to the
following for permission to reproduce copyright
material: p. 5, 8, 13, 21 Bettmann/Corbis; p. 6, 28
Corbis; p. 7, 15, 24, 29 The Granger Collection, New
York; p. 9, 19 top, 23, 25 North Wind Picture
Archives; p. 10, 14, 17, 19 bottom, 20, 22, 27 Peter
Newark's Military Pictures; p. 11 Delaware Art
Museum; p. 16, 26 Culver Pictures.

Cover photograph © The Granger Collection,
New York

**About the Author**
Diane Smolinski is a teacher for the Seminole
County School District in Florida. She earned B.S.
of Education degrees from Duquesne University and
Slippery Rock University in Pennsylvania. For the past
fourteen years, Diane has taught the Revolutionary
War curriculum to fourth and fifth graders. Diane
has previously authored a series of Civil War books
for young readers. She lives with her husband, two
daughters, and their cat, Pepper.

The author would like to thank the organizations,
historical societies, and reenactment groups that
maintain the historical sites, buildings, and museums
that make it possible for students to experience history.

**About the Consultant**
G.A. LoFaro is a lieutenant colonel in the U.S. Army
currently stationed at Fort McPherson, Georgia. After
graduating from West Point, he was commissioned in
the infantry. He has served in a variety of positions
in the 82nd Airborne Division, the Ranger Training
Brigade, and Second Infantry Division in Korea.
He has a Masters Degree in U.S. History from the
University of Michigan and is completing his Ph.D
in U.S. History at the State University of New York
at Stony Brook. He has also served six years on the
West Point faculty where he taught military history
to cadets.

Some words are shown in bold, **like this.**
You can find out what they mean by looking in the glossary.

# Contents

Battles of the Revolutionary War . . . . . . . . . . . . . . . . . .4

Lexington and Concord, Massachusetts . . . . . . . . . . . . .6

Bunker Hill, Massachusetts . . . . . . . . . . . . . . . . . . . . .8

Long Island, New York . . . . . . . . . . . . . . . . . . . . . . . .10

Trenton and Princeton, New Jersey . . . . . . . . . . . . . . .12

Brandywine and Germantown . . . . . . . . . . . . . . . . . . .14

Bennington, Vermont . . . . . . . . . . . . . . . . . . . . . . . . .16

Freeman's Farm . . . . . . . . . . . . . . . . . . . . . . . . . . . . .17

Bemis Heights and the Surrender at Saratoga . . . . . . .18

Monmouth Court House, New Jersey . . . . . . . . . . . . .20

The Southern Campaign . . . . . . . . . . . . . . . . . . . . . . .22

King's Mountain . . . . . . . . . . . . . . . . . . . . . . . . . . . . .24

Cowpens, South Carolina . . . . . . . . . . . . . . . . . . . . . .25

Guilford Court House . . . . . . . . . . . . . . . . . . . . . . . . .26

Yorktown, Virginia . . . . . . . . . . . . . . . . . . . . . . . . . . .27

Treaty of Paris . . . . . . . . . . . . . . . . . . . . . . . . . . . . . .28

*Glossary* . . . . . . . . . . . . . . . . . . . . . . . . . . . . . . . . . .*30*

*Historical Fiction to Read and Places to Visit* . . . . . . . . . . .*31*

*Index* . . . . . . . . . . . . . . . . . . . . . . . . . . . . . . . . . . . .*32*

# Battles of the Revolutionary War

From 1775 to 1783, North American **colonists** and the British Army fought each other for control of a land that was rich in raw materials and economic opportunities. The colonists were fighting for political freedom from British rule. This conflict was called the American Revolutionary War, or the American War of Independence.

The battles in this book were fought mainly on land and marked the beginning of the war, key turning points, and the end of the war. Many other battles not covered in this book were equally important in determining the final outcome of the Revolutionary War.

## Town Crier News

This war claimed the lives of more than 25,000 Americans. Battles claimed the lives of about 6,800 Americans. Other people died of other causes, such as disease.

*More than 1,500 **engagements** were fought during the 8 years of the war. The battles were fought in the area of North America that covers 27 present-day states and 3 Canadian provinces.*

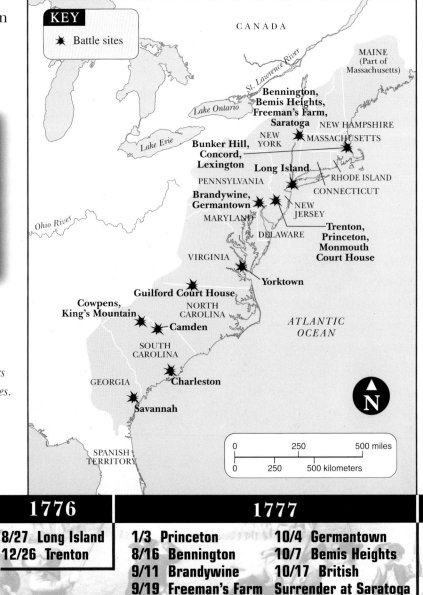

KEY

★ Battle sites

CANADA

St. Lawrence River

Lake Ontario

Lake Erie

Ohio River

MAINE (Part of Massachusetts)

NEW HAMPSHIRE

Bennington, Bemis Heights, Freeman's Farm, Saratoga

NEW YORK

MASSACHUSETTS

Bunker Hill, Concord, Lexington

Long Island

RHODE ISLAND

CONNECTICUT

PENNSYLVANIA

Brandywine, Germantown

NEW JERSEY

MARYLAND

DELAWARE

Trenton, Princeton, Monmouth Court House

VIRGINIA

Yorktown

Guilford Court House

Cowpens, King's Mountain

NORTH CAROLINA

Camden

ATLANTIC OCEAN

SOUTH CAROLINA

GEORGIA

Charleston

Savannah

SPANISH TERRITORY

N

| 0 | 250 | 500 miles |
| 0 | 250 | 500 kilometers |

| 1775 | 1776 | 1777 | |
|------|------|------|---|
| 4/19 Lexington and Concord | 8/27 Long Island | 1/3 Princeton | 10/4 Germantown |
| 6/17 Bunker Hill | 12/26 Trenton | 8/16 Bennington | 10/7 Bemis Heights |
| | | 9/11 Brandywine | 10/17 British |
| | | 9/19 Freeman's Farm | Surrender at Saratoga |

## Events Leading to the Revolutionary War

When the British finished fighting in the **French and Indian War** in 1763, the British government found itself in great debt. To raise money for payment of these war debts, **Parliament** passed laws that created taxes in the colonies. The taxes were also to help pay for having additional royal officials in the colonies. The Sugar Act, the Stamp Act, and the Tea Act were some of these laws. These acts called for additional taxes, which upset many North American colonists. They began to protest against them.

## Town Crier News

- The Sugar Act of 1764 taxed molasses shipped to the colonies. Molasses was the main sweetener used at the time.

- The Stamp Act of 1765 charged merchants a fee to stamp important papers with a government seal. Stamps had to be placed on documents such as newspapers, birth certificates, and wills.

In 1768, the British sent troops to Boston, Massachusetts, to stop colonial protests and restore order. But protests continued. In 1770, British troops shot five Americans in an event later called the Boston Massacre. Trying to regain control, the British Parliament passed the Intolerable Acts in 1774. These acts were meant to punish colonists who rebelled against British laws. In 1775, after much discussion, American and British government representatives were still not in agreement about taxes or political rights.

*Upset that Britain had sent troops to keep order in Boston, a group of colonists were yelling at some British soldiers. These troops fired into a crowd of colonists, killing five people. This event later was called the Boston Massacre.*

| 1778 | 1780 | 1781 | 1783 |
|------|------|------|------|
| 6/28 Monmouth Court House<br>12/29 Savannah | 4/11–5/12 Siege of Charleston<br>8/16 Camden<br>10/7 King's Mountain | 1/17 Cowpens<br>3/15 Guilford Court House<br>10/19 British surrender at Yorktown | 9/3 Treaty of Paris |

# Lexington and Concord, Massachusetts

**The British decided to use force to stop the colonists' activities in Massachusetts. General Thomas Gage, the British commander in chief, received orders to destroy the colonists' suspected ammunition storehouses in the town of Concord. Britain's professional soldiers expected to defeat the inexperienced colonial volunteers.**

On the evening of April 18, 1775, a group of 800 British troops crossed the Charles River in Boston and headed north toward Concord. **Patriots** Paul Revere and William Dawes also left Boston to warn colonists that the British were coming. When British troops arrived in the town of Lexington, about 70 Massachusetts **militiamen** stood ready to defend the town. Someone fired a shot. Musket fire killed eight militiamen and wounded ten. Only one British soldier was killed, and the British continued to march west to Concord.

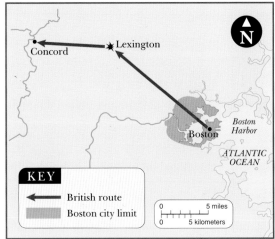

*British troops marched about 15 miles (24 kilometers) from Boston to Lexington and then another 9 miles (14.5 kilometers) to Concord.*

## After Action Report—Lexington

|  | Continental Army | British Army |
| --- | --- | --- |
| **Military Leaders** | Captain John Parker | Lt. Col. Francis Smith |
| **Troop Strength** | about 70 militiamen | 800 |
| ***Casualties** | 18 | 1 |
| **Outcome** | defeat | victory |

\* Casualties include those who were wounded, killed, or missing in action. These figures are unavailable for some Revolutionary War battles, because the people involved did not always keep records of the numbers.

**1775**     **1776**     **1777**

**4/19 Lexington and Concord**

## Concord

When the British Army arrived in Concord, it searched the town for ammunition storehouses but found that most of the ammunition had been removed. The troops then marched to the surrounding fields. Local militiamen were waiting for them there, and shots were fired. The British soldiers retreated to the town and decided to return to Boston. On the way, they met a troop of British **reinforcements** that had come to help. Together they fought the local militia all the way back to Boston, Massachusetts.

*The British marched in straight and close rows called columns. Here, troops are retreating from Concord, Massachusetts.*

## Battle Aftermath

Massachusetts now asked neighboring colonies to join them in fighting the British. Within two months, about 15,000 militiamen from all over New England came and built **fortifications** around Boston. They still needed supplies, training, and equipment. The British Army in Boston numbered only about 6,500 soldiers. But they were well supplied, well trained, had proper equipment, and had a powerful navy to support them. They were ready for the battle to control the city of Boston.

### Town Crier News

British troops left Concord when they discovered that most of the supplies they came to get had been removed. Marching back to Boston, they came under "guerrilla warfare" attacks by the colonial militiamen. Militiamen hid behind trees, stone walls, homes, and wood piles along the route and fired on passing columns of British troops.

### After Action Report—Concord and British Retreat

|  | Continental Army | British Army |
|---|---|---|
| **Military Leaders** | Col. James Barrett | Lt. Col. Francis Smith |
| **Troop Strength** | about 3,800 militia | 800 plus 1,000 reinforcements |
| **Casualties** | 95 | 286 |
| **Outcome** | victory | defeat |

1778     1780     1781     1783

# Bunker Hill, Massachusetts

On the night of June 15 and into the early morning of June 16, 1775, **colonial militiamen** positioned themselves on Breed's Hill on the **peninsula** across the bay from Boston. General Thomas Gage, the British commander in chief, planned to move some of his British troops to the eastern end of the peninsula and to push the colonial troops back to the mainland.

The British barges and boats landed, and disciplined lines of foot soldiers attacked. Warships and **artillery** supported them. The colonial troops stood their ground on the first two attacks, but ran out of ammunition and had no **reinforcements** coming. British reinforcements arrived, and they attacked a third time. The British successfully drove the militiamen from the peninsula. The battle is seen as a colonial victory, however, because so many British troops were killed or wounded during the **engagement.**

*The battle was called Bunker Hill, but it actually was fought on Breed's Hill. Because the battle was at night, the soldiers made a mistake and thought Breed's Hill was Bunker Hill.*

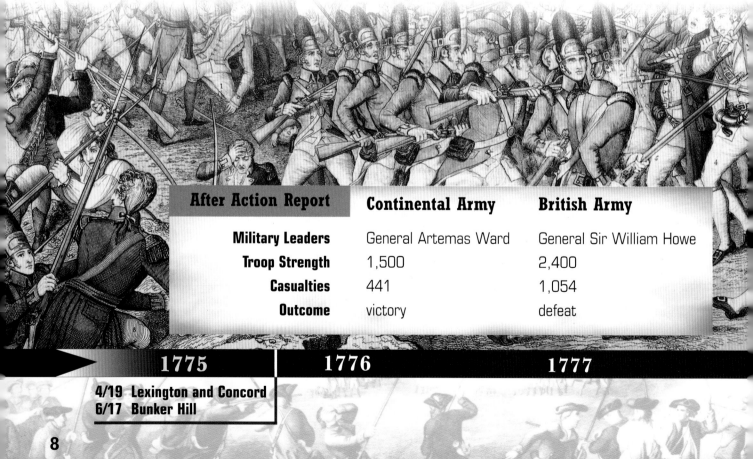

| After Action Report | Continental Army | British Army |
| --- | --- | --- |
| Military Leaders | General Artemas Ward | General Sir William Howe |
| Troop Strength | 1,500 | 2,400 |
| Casualties | 441 | 1,054 |
| Outcome | victory | defeat |

**1775**    **1776**    **1777**

**4/19 Lexington and Concord**
**6/17 Bunker Hill**

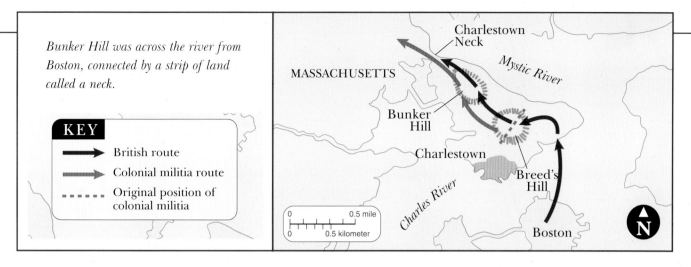

*Bunker Hill was across the river from Boston, connected by a strip of land called a neck.*

MASSACHUSETTS

Charlestown Neck

Mystic River

Bunker Hill

Charlestown

Breed's Hill

Charles River

Boston

**KEY**

→ British route

→ Colonial militia route

- - - - Original position of colonial militia

0    0.5 mile
0    0.5 kilometer

N

## Battle Aftermath

Both sides realized that they needed larger armies. The British increased the size of their army by hiring **foreign troops,** which was common at this time. The colonists had to rely on volunteers because they did not have money to hire professional soldiers. They needed a regular, trained army. In June 1775, the Second **Continental Congress** agreed to form a Continental Army and appointed General George Washington the commander in chief.

## Preparing for the Next Battle

While fighting continued in parts of Canada and in the southern colonies, the Continental Army forced the British out of Boston on March 17, 1776. The British Army then went to Nova Scotia in Canada to gather supplies and equipment before heading for New York. General Washington's Continental Army also moved from Boston to New York.

*Almost 17,000 soldiers from the German state of Hesse Cassel came to help the British fight the colonists. Britain paid the prince of this German state for the use of his soldiers.*

## Town Crier News

Before the regular Continental Army was formed, each colony had a military force called a militia. All physically fit men between the ages of 16 and 60 were to be a part of their state militia. Militiamen usually had to provide their own equipment and uniforms since individual colonies often did not have enough money to provide supplies.

1778        1780        1781        1783

# Long Island, New York

**New York City was an important harbor and business center within the North American colonies. For that reason, the British Army decided to make it their headquarters.**

General Washington positioned much of his army on Long Island to protect New York City from a British attack. State militias joined the Continental Army. Meanwhile, British ships moved troops from Staten Island to Long Island. Both armies prepared their **infantry** and light field **artillery.** The British also had their powerful navy to back them up.

*British troops from the south joined General Howe's forces at Long Island. Admiral Richard Howe, William Howe's brother, positioned a strong British Navy to back up the infantry.*

*Troops were placed in three major locations—on Manhattan Island, Long Island, and the New Jersey side of the Hudson River.*

**KEY**
→ Path of British troops
→ Path of American troops (Continental Army & state militias)
- - - Original position of most of Washington's Army

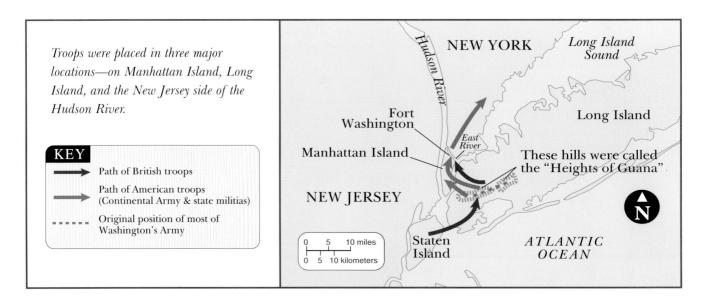

NEW YORK
Hudson River
Long Island Sound
Fort Washington
East River
Long Island
Manhattan Island
These hills were called the "Heights of Guana"
NEW JERSEY
N
0  5  10 miles
0  5  10 kilometers
Staten Island
ATLANTIC OCEAN

**1775**    **1776**    **1777**

4/19 Lexington and Concord
6/17 Bunker Hill

8/27 Long Island

*Washington's troops retreat through New Jersey.*

General William Howe's army surprised the inexperienced colonial troops and overpowered them. Washington's army was forced to retreat by boat across the East River back to Manhattan. But some Continental troops continued north, and the British did not chase them. Other colonial soldiers stayed on Manhattan Island to hold Fort Washington. The British eventually did capture the fort, putting them in control of Manhattan Island.

## Battle Aftermath

By September 1776, British troops controlled all of New York City and would continue to do so for the rest of the war. Determined to recover other British territories, the British Army continued to win battles in the colonies of New York, New Jersey, and Rhode Island. After losing battle after battle, many Continental soldiers wanted to go home. General Washington needed to find a way to encourage soldiers to stay in the army.

| After Action Report | Continental Army | British Army |
| --- | --- | --- |
| Military Leaders | Gen. George Washington | Gen. Sir William Howe |
| Troop Strength | 3,500 | 20,000 |
| Casualties | 1,000 | 370 |
| Outcome | defeat | victory |

1778          1780          1781          1783

# Trenton and Princeton, New Jersey

**On December 25, 1776, the Delaware River was filled with chunks of ice. That cold, winter evening, about 2,400 of General Washington's troops, with 18 cannons, rowed across the river into New Jersey.**

Once the troops landed, they still had to march nearly nine miles (14.4 kilometers) to reach the city of Trenton. They approached from two different routes, and early the next morning they surprised the **Hessian** soldiers in the town. Their muskets and **artillery** were soaked from the freezing rain, so **bayonets** were used in the battle. The Hessians surrendered, and more than 900 prisoners were taken back across the Delaware River and marched through Philadelphia. The inexperienced **colonial** volunteers had defeated professional soldiers.

## Town Crier News

- A total of 29,166 soldiers came from Germany to fight in the Revolutionary War for the British.

- German soldiers were often called Hessians. That was because almost 17,000 of the German soldiers were from the German provinces of Hesse Cassel and Hesse Hanau.

## On to Princeton

A week later, the Continental soldiers again crossed the Delaware River near Trenton. By this time, Lord Cornwallis was on his way to meet them with British troops, but he was too late. The colonial army defeated the **garrison** at Princeton. The outnumbered, but successful, Continental Army then retreated into the western part of New Jersey to rest for the winter.

### After Action Report—Trenton

| | Continental Army | British Army |
| --- | --- | --- |
| **Military Leaders** | General George Washington | Hessian Colonel Johann Rall |
| **Troop Strength** | 2,400 | 1,400 |
| **Casualties** | 4 wounded | 114 casualties<br>948 captured |
| **Outcome** | victory | defeat |

| 1775 | 1776 | 1777 |
| --- | --- | --- |
| 4/19 **Lexington and Concord**<br>6/17 **Bunker Hill** | 8/27 **Long Island**<br>12/26 **Trenton** | 1/3 **Princeton** |

The Continental Army surprised the British by attacking in winter. George Washington and his troops crossed the Delaware River by night, despite the icy conditions.

## Battles Aftermath

Victories at Trenton and Princeton gave men a reason to join the Continental Army. To encourage even more soldiers to sign up, colonies offered **bounties,** passed **conscription** laws, and allowed substitutes. The British withdrew from most of New Jersey. General Sir William Howe stayed in his winter quarters in New York City through the spring. He was now determined to control Philadelphia.

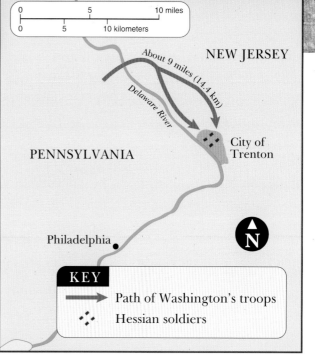

Colonial troops traveled to Trenton after crossing the Delaware.

| After Action Report—Princeton | | |
| --- | --- | --- |
| | **Continental Army** | **British Army** |
| **Military Leaders** | General George Washington | General Lord Charles Cornwallis |
| **Troop Strength** | 1,600 | 1,200 |
| **Casualties** | 40 | 275 |
| **Outcome** | victory | defeat |

1778     1780     1781     1783

# Brandywine and Germantown

**In 1777, Philadelphia, Pennsylvania, was the largest city in North America, having more than 30,000 people. The British did not want the Continental Army to control this supply base.**

## Brandywine

In June, General Sir William Howe left New York City. He tried to engage General Washington's troops in a battle near New Jersey, but failed. He then sailed his troops toward Philadelphia, landed his army in Maryland, and marched north. General Washington led his troops south through Philadelphia. Howe then sent **Hessian** troops to attack the center of Washington's battle line. Howe and General Charles Cornwallis—who was serving under Howe—crossed Brandywine Creek and attacked the right side of Washington's line. As darkness fell, the tired Continental troops retreated. The victory at Brandywine went to the British.

| After Action Report—Brandywine | | |
|---|---|---|
| | **Continental Army** | **British Army** |
| **Military Leaders** | Gen. George Washington | Gen. Sir William Howe |
| **Troop Strength** | 11,000 | 25,000 |
| **Casualties** | 1,200 | 600 |
| **Outcome** | defeat | victory |

*The Continental Army was outnumbered by the British at the Battle of Brandywine.*

| ► | 1775 | 1776 | 1777 | |
|---|---|---|---|---|
| | 4/19 Lexington and Concord | 8/27 Long Island | 1/3 Princeton | 10/4 Germantown |
| | 6/17 Bunker Hill | 12/26 Trenton | 9/11 Brandywine | |

General Howe then led his troops west of Philadelphia. Over the next few weeks, a number of smaller battles took place. Then the British marched into and captured an undefended Philadelphia.

## Surprise Attack at Germantown

Most of the British Army camped five miles (eight kilometers) north of Philadelphia in a town named Germantown. Even though his troops were still inexperienced compared to the British, Washington tried a surprise attack. The battle seemed to go well for the **Patriots** at first, but the British pulled together and gained strength. As thick fog caused confusion, the **colonial** troops fell back. In November, the Continental Army finally gave up its defensive positions around Philadelphia.

*During the Battle of Germantown, the colonists attacked a house that the British were using as headquarters.*

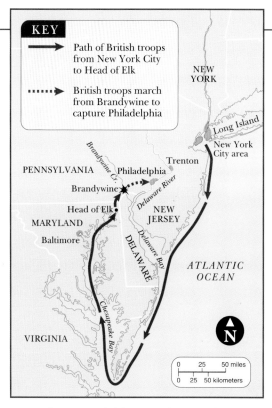

*General Howe sailed his British troops from New York City to the town of Head of Elk, Maryland. After landing, they marched north to Brandywine. Today, Head of Elk is called Elkton, Maryland.*

*Washington's army suffered about 1,073 casualties. The British casualties numbered about 550.*

1778     1780          1781          1783

# Bennington, Vermont

In June 1777, British General John Burgoyne left Quebec, Canada, for Albany, New York. The British wanted to separate the New England **colonies** so that they would not be able to help each other. Burgoyne planned to attack from the north, and General Howe would attack from the south. They hoped to trap the Continental Army in between. The orders did not reach General Howe in time, however, and he did not move his army into position. The plan failed.

*General Burgoyne*

## Destination—Albany, New York

As Burgoyne traveled south, he recaptured Fort Ticonderoga. Some of his troops chased the colonial troops who left the fort. Others sailed on Lake Champlain toward Albany. The wilderness made it difficult to move troops. **Reinforcements** failed to arrive, and supplies were not delivered. Burgoyne sent 800 soldiers to find food and equipment. On August 16, 1777, the New Hampshire and Vermont militias surprised the British at Bennington, Vermont, and nearly wiped out the search party. The British force grew smaller.

*Forts often guarded important positions on waterways. Fort Ticonderoga near Lake Champlain in New York was one such fort. It was built by the French in 1756 and called Fort Carillon. The British captured it in 1759 and renamed it Fort Ticonderoga.*

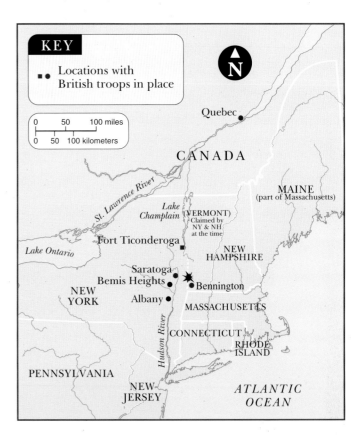

**KEY**

■ • Locations with British troops in place

0   50   100 miles
0   50   100 kilometers

Quebec

CANADA

*St. Lawrence River*

MAINE
(part of Massachusetts)

Lake Champlain

(VERMONT)
Claimed by
NY & NH
at the time

Lake Ontario

Fort Ticonderoga

NEW HAMPSHIRE

Saratoga
Bemis Heights

Bennington

NEW YORK

Albany

MASSACHUSETTS

*Hudson River*

CONNECTICUT

RHODE ISLAND

PENNSYLVANIA

NEW JERSEY

ATLANTIC OCEAN

| 1775 | 1776 | 1777 | |
|---|---|---|---|
| 4/19 Lexington and Concord | 8/27 Long Island | 1/3 Princeton | 9/19 Freeman's Farm |
| 6/17 Bunker Hill | 12/26 Trenton | 8/16 Bennington | 10/4 Germantown |
| | | 9/11 Brandywine | |

# Freeman's Farm

**Burgoyne crossed the Hudson River near Saratoga, New York, and continued toward Albany. General Horatio Gates positioned his colonial troops on Bemis Heights and blocked the road from Saratoga to Albany.**

Burgoyne's troops advanced toward the colonial line. General Gates's troops stayed on Bemis Heights, while troops under Benedict Arnold moved forward to meet the advancing British Army at Freeman's Farm. Soldiers fought with rifles, muskets, light **artillery,** and **bayonets.** Reinforcements came for the colonial troops, but not for the British. Even so, the British managed to gain control of the battlefield. But many lives were lost, many men were injured, and British troops still had not reached Albany.

*As backup for the battle at Freeman's Farm, General Gates positioned Continental troops at Bemis Heights to keep the British Army from advancing any farther toward Albany.*

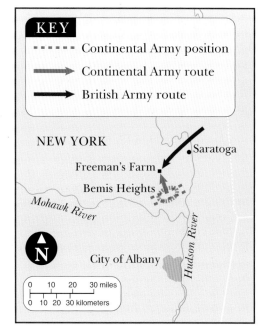

**KEY**

- - - - - Continental Army position
——▶ Continental Army route
━━▶ British Army route

NEW YORK

Saratoga

Freeman's Farm

Bemis Heights

Mohawk River

City of Albany

Hudson River

| 0 | 10 | 20 | 30 miles |
| 0 | 10 | 20 | 30 kilometers |

*This map shows the placement of Continental troops and the advancement of both armies, leading up to the surrender at Saratoga.*

1778     1780          1781          1783

# Bemis Heights and the Surrender at Saratoga

While Burgoyne's troops waited for help from General Henry Clinton, their rations were running out. Clinton started to bring troops to help Burgoyne, capturing several forts along the way. However, Clinton began to worry about how long he had been away from New York City. He decided to turn back to protect his headquarters.

Burgoyne decided not to wait any longer for Clinton's help. He took part of his army and attacked Bemis Heights. The **colonial** troops were ready for them, however. Colonial **militiamen** had joined General Horatio Gates's forces on Bemis Heights, and together they destroyed the British force. The rest of Burgoyne's army withdrew. The colonial troops had succeeded in stopping the British march to Albany. They chased the British up the Hudson River and surrounded them. On October 17, 1777, Burgoyne surrendered his entire army at Saratoga.

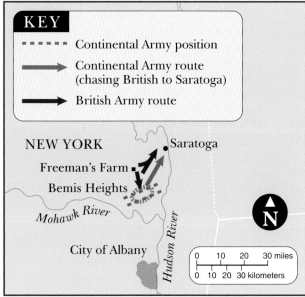

*The Continental Army chased British troops from Bemis Heights to Saratoga.*

## After Action Report—Surrender at Saratoga

|  | Continental Army | British Army |
| --- | --- | --- |
| **Military Leaders** | General Horatio Gates | General John Burgoyne |
| **Troop Strength** | 17,000 | 5,728 |
| **Casualties** | 500 | 1,200 |
| **Outcome** | victory | defeat (full surrender) |

| 1775 | 1776 | 1777 | |
| --- | --- | --- | --- |
| 4/19 Lexington and Concord | 8/27 Long Island | 1/3 Princeton | 10/4 Germantown |
| 6/17 Bunker Hill | 12/26 Trenton | 8/16 Bennington | 10/7 Bemis Heights |
| | | 9/11 Brandywine | 10/17 British |
| | | 9/19 Freeman's Farm | Surrender at Saratoga |

## Battle Aftermath

After the victory at Saratoga, France became an **ally** of the colonies. The French sent troops, money, and naval support. The British plan to separate the New England colonies had failed. The colonial troops had defeated the efforts of the professional British Army, and **Patriot** confidence in the Continental Army grew.

Over the next two years, the British tried to hold their remaining positions in the colonies. At the same time, they sent troops and ships to fight the French, Spanish, and Dutch in other parts of the world to protect their political and economic interests. During this period, the British decided to move their headquarters from Philadelphia to New York City. But to get there, they had to march through New Jersey and fight the Continental Army.

*British General Burgoyne offers his sword in surrender to General Gates. Burgoyne went back to England after surrendering at Saratoga. This surrender was an embarrassment for the British. Because of this, Burgoyne never commanded troops in the British Army again.*

## Town Crier News

- In February of 1778, Benjamin Franklin and other Patriots met with the King of France, Louis the Sixteenth (Louis XVI).

- In a document called The Treaty of Alliance, France agreed to help the Patriots fight the British in the American Revolutionary War.

*During the Revolutionary War, French ships battled the British Navy.*

1778     1780     1781     1783

# Monmouth Court House, New Jersey

On June 18, 1778, British troops left Philadelphia and headed for New York City. Too many ships would have been needed to transfer all of the British troops, **Loyalists,** and equipment by sea. So the British sent Loyalists and some supplies by ship, but the army and **artillery** marched north. They expected to meet the Continental Army in New Jersey.

### An Improved Continental Army

Washington's Continental Army had spent the winter training at Valley Forge, Pennsylvania, under Baron Friedrich von Steuben, a former soldier in the German Army. He taught the Continental Army how to fight in disciplined columns and lines and how to use **bayonets.** These improved skills gave Washington's army the confidence to fight the more experienced British troops.

*Baron von Steuben was appointed Inspector General in charge of training the Continental Army. He was to help them become a strong force against the British Army.*

## Town Crier News

- Baron von Steuben spoke very little English.

- He wrote a manual of arms, a training book, for the Continental troops at Valley Forge.

| 1775 | 1776 | 1777 | |
|------|------|------|--|
| 4/19 Lexington and Concord | 8/27 Long Island | 1/3 Princeton | 10/4 Germantown |
| 6/17 Bunker Hill | 12/26 Trenton | 8/16 Bennington | 10/7 Bemis Heights |
| | | 9/11 Brandywine | 10/17 British |
| | | 9/19 Freeman's Farm | Surrender at Saratoga |

## Town Crier News

The Battle of Monmouth Court House was fought during a heat wave. Molly Pitcher, whose real name was Mary Ludwig Hays McCauley, is said to have taken water to thirsty Continental soldiers.

## British Return to New York City

Washington's Continental Army faced Clinton's British Army in New Jersey. The Continental Army first attacked Clinton's rear guard. The British response was stronger than expected, however, so the Continental Army pulled back to get organized. General Washington sent his troops forward again and the Continental Army held their line. A fierce battle lasted throughout the day until darkness fell. Neither side could claim a victory. During the night, the British pulled out and continued their march to New York City.

## Battle Aftermath

With the help of the French Navy, the **colonial** troops decided to attack a British fort in Rhode Island. This was the first time in the war that the French and the Americans planned to combine forces. Unfortunately, a storm prevented the French Navy from reaching the fort. The colonial troops did not think they could fight the British alone, so they withdrew.

*Molly Pitcher's husband fired a cannon for the Continental Army. When he was wounded during the Battle of Monmouth, Molly took his place at the cannon.*

1778     1780     1781     1783

6/28 Monmouth Court House

# The Southern Campaign

After nearly two years of fighting, the British still had not been able to end the **rebellion** in the **colonies.** In 1778, the British decided that they needed to control the southern colonies of Georgia, South Carolina, and North Carolina. After bringing them back under British rule, they could use these colonies as bases from which to regain control of the ten remaining colonies. This plan required the strength of their navy and the help of southern **Loyalists.**

## Battle for Georgia

In November 1778, Lieutenant Colonel Archibald Campbell sailed from New York City with 3,500 British soldiers. In December, near Savannah, Georgia, he defeated a force of 1,000 **militiamen** led by General Robert Howe. After the fall of Savannah, the British went on to capture the city of Augusta. Having gained control of Georgia, the British now turned their attention to South Carolina.

## Disasters for the Colonial Troops

The Continental Army was positioned in Charleston, South Carolina, an important military base and port. British Navy ships were positioned along the coast, and the British Army surrounded Charleston while their **reinforcements** arrived nearby. The **siege** lasted about a month before the outnumbered colonial troops surrendered and lost control of this important port city. They also surrendered about 5,000 troops and large amounts of **artillery,** guns, and ammunition.

*Casimir Pulaski, an experienced soldier from Poland, volunteered to help the Continental Army. While fighting the British at Savannah, General Pulaski was shot. He later died from the injury.*

| 1775 | 1776 | 1777 | |
|---|---|---|---|
| 4/19 Lexington and Concord | 8/27 Long Island | 1/3 Princeton | 10/4 Germantown |
| 6/17 Bunker Hill | 12/26 Trenton | 8/16 Bennington | 10/7 Bemis Heights |
| | | 9/11 Brandywine | 10/17 British |
| | | 9/19 Freeman's Farm | Surrender at Saratoga |

## Battle Aftermath

After Charleston, the British plan to establish control in South Carolina was blocked by repeated local militia attacks. The newly appointed commander of the Southern Continental Army, General Horatio Gates, decided to attack the British **outpost** at Camden. The British surprised colonial forces, however, by attacking first and killing or capturing nearly half of their 4,000 troops.

*Colonial troops fought to defend the harbor in Charleston, South Carolina.*

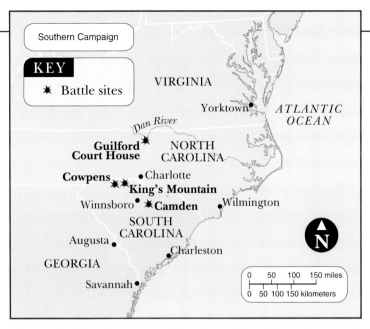

*The British planned to capture the major southern cities, gain control of the countryside, and then move north to recapture colonial cities.*

### After Action Report—Camden, South Carolina

|  | **Continental Army** | **British Army** |
| --- | --- | --- |
| **Military Leaders** | General Horatio Gates | General Charles Cornwallis |
| **Troop Strength** | 4,000 | 2,100 |
| **Casualties** | nearly 1,800 | 324 |
| **Outcome** | defeat | victory |

## Town Crier News

- Savannah was the capital of Georgia during the Revolutionary War.

- There were 137 **engagements** in South Carolina during the Revolutionary War.

| 1778 | 1780 | 1781 | 1783 |
| --- | --- | --- | --- |
| **6/28 Monmouth Court House** **12/29 Savannah** | **4/11–5/12 Siege of Charleston** **8/16 Camden** | | |

*Turning Point in the South for Colonial Troops*     *October 7, 1780*

# King's Mountain

Even after victories at Charleston and Camden, the British could not control the South Carolina countryside. Lord Charles Cornwallis then decided to invade North Carolina. He hoped to find more **Loyalists** to help the British gain control of South Carolina. Cornwallis broke his army into two parts. One part, under Major Patrick Ferguson, traveled farther west to find Loyalists who could help. Cornwallis led the other part on a different route. The two groups were to meet near Charlotte.

Near the North Carolina–South Carolina border, Ferguson's group, made up entirely of Loyalists, camped on King's Mountain. On October 7, 1780, a group of North Carolina **Patriots** went up the mountain and surrounded Ferguson's group. In the fighting that followed, they killed Ferguson and killed or captured most of his British force.

King's Mountain was the first significant Patriot victory in the South since the fall of Savannah. Southern Patriots continued to attack Loyalist forces and kept the British from gaining complete control of South Carolina. Francis Marion, nicknamed the "Swamp Fox," was the best known of these Patriots.

*Francis Marion, the "Swamp Fox," leads several boats of Patriots across the Pee Dee River in South Carolina.*

## Town Crier News

- Francis Marion was nicknamed the "Swamp Fox" by the British because of his ability to attack their troops and then disappear quickly into the swamps.

- Marion helped keep the British Army from controlling the Carolina countryside.

| 1775 | 1776 | 1777 | |
|------|------|------|---|
| 4/19 Lexington and Concord | 8/27 Long Island | 1/3 Princeton | 10/4 Germantown |
| 6/17 Bunker Hill | 12/26 Trenton | 8/16 Bennington | 10/7 Bemis Heights |
| | | 9/11 Brandywine | 10/17 British |
| | | 9/19 Freeman's Farm | Surrender at Saratoga |

24

# Cowpens, South Carolina

**After the British defeat at King's Mountain, Cornwallis gave up his plan to invade North Carolina. He withdrew to Winnsboro, South Carolina, to spend the winter and wait for reinforcements.**

General Nathanael Greene became the new commander of the Continental forces in the South. Greene split his army into two groups. General Daniel Morgan headed one, and the other was under Greene's command. General Morgan had been collecting supplies and recruiting militia from the backcountry of South Carolina.

Cornwallis sent troops, led by Lieutenant Colonel Banastre Tarleton, to stop Morgan. These two groups met in battle at Cowpens. Morgan placed two lines of local **militiamen** in front of disciplined and skilled Continental troops. When the British attacked, the militia fired two **volleys,** then retreated. These volleys slowed the British charge. Fresh Continental troops then attacked the broken British line. Tarleton's troops, already exhausted from a long march, were defeated.

*Banastre Tarleton led his men in hand-to-hand combat against Continental troops at the Battle of Cowpens. The Continental Army forced Tarleton's troops to retreat to the British camp.*

| After Action Report | Continental Army | British Army |
| --- | --- | --- |
| Military Leaders | General Daniel Morgan | Lt. Colonel Banastre Tarleton |
| Troop Strength | 320 Continental Army 720 militiamen | 1,100 |
| Casualties | 72 | 990 |
| Outcome | victory | defeat |

| 1778 | 1780 | 1781 | 1783 |
| --- | --- | --- | --- |
| 6/28 Monmouth Court House 12/29 Savannah | 4/11–5/12 Siege of Charleston 8/16 Camden 10/7 King's Mountain | 1/17 Cowpens | |

# Guilford Court House

General Cornwallis and his British troops advanced into North Carolina to fight Nathanael Greene's forces. When Cornwallis heard about Tarleton's defeat at Cowpens, he was determined to destroy the **colonial** troops. The two colonial groups under Greene and Morgan came together and retreated northward. Cornwallis chased them. The British troops became tired and weak from following the retreat of the colonial troops. When the colonial troops crossed the Dan River in Virginia, the British did not follow. Instead, they returned south to North Carolina.

Nathanael Greene, now in charge of both colonial forces, carefully followed the British. **Reinforcements** for the colonial troops arrived near the town of Guilford Court House. Now the **Patriot** force was about twice as large as the British force. Colonial troops set up their position, and the British attacked.

At the end of the day, Cornwallis controlled the battlefield, but his army had suffered great losses. They needed reinforcements. He took his troops to Wilmington, North Carolina, on the coast to regroup. Cornwallis then decided to take over Virginia, in hopes of ending the war in the South. He began his march to Virginia to meet his reinforcements.

*The colonial cavalry gets ready for the Battle at Guilford Court House.*

| After Action Report | Continental Army | British Army |
|---|---|---|
| Military Leaders | Gen. Nathanael Greene | Gen. Charles Cornwallis |
| Troop Strength | 4,400 | 1,900 |
| Casualties | 260 | 532 |
| Outcome | defeat | victory |

| 1775 | 1776 | 1777 | |
|---|---|---|---|
| 4/19 Lexington and Concord | 8/27 Long Island | 1/3 Princeton | 10/4 Germantown |
| 6/17 Bunker Hill | 12/26 Trenton | 8/16 Bennington | 10/7 Bemis Heights |
| | | 9/11 Brandywine | 10/17 British |
| | | 9/19 Freeman's Farm | Surrender at Saratoga |

# Yorktown, Virginia

General Washington and the French Army combined their forces for a total of about 16,000 troops. The French Navy was also on its way to help the Continental Army. Cornwallis had fewer than 8,000 British troops, and his reinforcements never arrived. The Continental and French armies bombarded British troops day and night. Colonial forces killed or captured the British troops at Yorktown. The only other British troops left in the colonies were in New York.

The British were also fighting the French, Spanish, and Dutch in the West Indies. They did not have any more soldiers available to send as reinforcements to the colonies. The British were forced to surrender to the Continental Army.

| After Action Report | Continental Army | British Army |
| --- | --- | --- |
| Military Leaders | General Rochambeau | General Charles Cornwallis |
| Troop Strength | 16,000 | fewer than 8,000 |
| Casualties | 262 | unknown |
| Outcome | victory | defeat |

*Together, the Continental and French Armies overpowered the British Army at Yorktown.*

| 1778 | 1780 | 1781 | 1783 |
| --- | --- | --- | --- |
| 6/28 Monmouth Court House<br>12/29 Savannah | 4/11–5/12 Siege of Charleston<br>8/16 Camden<br>10/7 King's Mountain | 1/17 Cowpens<br>3/15 Guilford Court House<br>10/19 British surrender at Yorktown | |

# Treaty of Paris

**After Yorktown, minor battles continued for eighteen more months before peace talks began. After eight years of war, peace negotiations took place in Paris, France.**

John Adams, Benjamin Franklin, and John Jay represented the American **colonies** at the negotiations. David Hartley and Richard Oswald, the chief negotiator, represented Great Britain. An initial agreement was reached late in 1782 and signed on September 3, 1783 officially ending the Revolutionary War.

## Town Crier News

- On the same day, Great Britain also signed separate treaties with France and Spain in the city of Versailles, France.

- The **Continental Congress** in the United States had to approve the treaty after it was signed in Paris. It had to be approved and sent back to England within six months.

- The Continental Congress finally approved the terms of the treaty on January 14, 1784.

*As each man signed the Treaty of Paris, he pressed his personal symbol into red wax. This showed that the signature was really his.*

| 1775 | 1776 | 1777 | |
|---|---|---|---|
| 4/19 Lexington and Concord | 8/27 Long Island | 1/3 Princeton | 10/4 Germantown |
| 6/17 Bunker Hill | 12/26 Trenton | 8/16 Bennington | 10/7 Bemis Heights |
| | | 9/11 Brandywine | 10/17 British |
| | | 9/19 Freeman's Farm | Surrender at Saratoga |

## Terms of the Treaty

Colonial independence from Great Britain finally was recognized. The northern border with Canada stayed the same, but several new national boundaries were established. The Mississippi River became the boundary in the west, and Spain received Florida and parts of Alabama and Mississippi. Congress asked each state to allow the **Loyalists** to return home and live on their properties.

Britain was forced to give up its North American colonies. This was an economic loss for the British. The war brought independence for the United States and forced the development of a national army and navy. The challenge ahead would be to grow as an independent nation.

*Once the British had left New York City on November 25, 1783, the American flag was flown high above New York Harbor to celebrate.*

| 1778 | 1780 | 1781 | 1783 |
|------|------|------|------|
| 6/28 Monmouth Court House<br>12/29 Savannah | 4/11–5/12 Siege of Charleston<br>8/16 Camden<br>10/7 King's Mountain | 1/17 Cowpens<br>3/15 Guilford Court House<br>10/19 British surrender at Yorktown | 9/3 Treaty of Paris |

# Glossary

**ally**  political supporter, particularly in a time of war

**artillery**  cannons

**bayonet**  long, pointed knife that attached to the end of a musket or rifle

**bounty**  reward paid by a government to those who join the military

**colony**  territory settled by people from other countries who still had loyalty to those other countries. The word *colonist* is used to describe a person who lives in a colony. The word *colonial* is used to describe things related to a colony.

**conscription**  law that required men to join the military

**Continental Congress**  group of representatives from the colonies that carried out the duties of the government

**engagement**  any fighting occurring during a war

**foreign troops**  groups of soldiers who came from other countries to fight in the American Revolutionary War

**fortification**  structure built to protect soldiers from an attacking group

**French and Indian War**  called the Seven Years' War in Europe. From 1754 to 1763, Britain fought against France in the North American colonies. Some Native Americans—called Indians at the time—helped the French.

**garrison**  military post or fort

**Hessian**  soldier from the German states of Hesse Cassel and Hesse Hanan who fought for the British in the American Revolutionary War

**infantry**  foot soldiers in an army

**Loyalist**  colonist who supported the British government during the American Revolution

**militiaman**  man who joined a small military unit organized by an individual state to defend a local community

**negotiation**  working out an agreement between two or more people or groups

**outpost**  small military fort

**Parliament**  lawmakers of the British government

**Patriot**  person during colonial times who believed that the colonies should break away from the rule of Great Britain and form their own government

**peninsula**  land nearly surrounded by water and connected to a larger body of land by a thin piece of land

**rebellion**  act of trying to overthrow a legal government

**reinforcements**  troops brought to help an army under attack

**siege**  to surround an opposing army and capture it by bombing and blockading it

**volley**  many weapons firing at the same time

# Historical Fiction to Read

Denenberg, Barry. *The Journal of William Thomas Emerson: A Revolutionary War Patriot:*
*Boston, Massachusetts, 1774.* New York: Scholastic, 1998.
A twelve-year-old orphan boy keeps a diary of his experiences before and during the
Revolutionary War.

Gregory, Kristiana. *The Winter of Red Snow: The Revolutionary War Diary of Abigail Jane Stewart,*
*Valley Forge, Pennsylvania, 1777.* New York: Scholastic, 1996.
A young girl living close to the military camp at Valley Forge writes in her diary about the
things she sees.

Osborne, Mary Pope. *Revolutionary War on Wednesday.* New York: Random House, 2000.
Travel back in time to the Revolutionary War to help General Washington during the
crossing of the Delaware River.

# Historical Places to Visit

**Colonial National Historical Park**
P.O. Box 210
Yorktown, Virginia 23690
Visitor Information: (757) 898-2410
Visit Yorktown, the site of the last major battle of the Revolutionary War in 1781.

**Cowpens National Battlefield**
4001 Chesnee Highway
Chesnee, South Carolina 29323
Visitor Information: (864) 461-2828
Visit the site of the Continental victory at Cowpens. See where General Daniel Morgan's
troops defeated Lieutenant Colonel Banastre Tarleton's British regulars on January 17, 1781.

**Minute Man National Historical Park**
174 Liberty Street
Concord, Massachusetts 01742
Visitor Information: (978) 369-6993
This park stretches across the historic sites of some of the opening battles of the
Revolutionary war. Visit the sites of the battles at Concord, Lincoln, and Lexington.

**Saratoga National Historical Park**
648 Route 32
Still Water, New York 12170
Visitor Information: (518) 664-9821, extension 224
Visit the site of one of the most important battles of the Revolutionary War. See the place
where, in 1777, the British Army surrendered to Continental forces.

# Index

Arnold, Benedict   17

Bemis Heights, Battle of   17–18
Bennington, Battle of   16
Boston Massacre   5
Brandywine, Battle of   14
Breed's Hill   8
Bunker Hill, Battle of   8–9
Burgoyne, General John   16–18, 19

Camden, South Carolina   23, 24
Campbell, Lieutenant Colonel Archibald   22
Charleston, siege of   22–23
Clinton, General Henry   18, 21
Concord, Massachusetts   6, 7
Continental Congress   9, 28
Cornwallis, Lord Charles   12, 14, 24–27
Cowpens, Battle of   25, 26

Dawes, William   6

Ferguson, Major Patrick   24
Franklin, Benjamin   19
Freeman's Farm, Battle of   17
French   19, 21, 27
French and Indian War   5

Gage, General Thomas   6
Gates, General Horatio   17–18, 19, 23
Germantown, Battle of   15
Greene, General Nathanael   25–26
Guilford Court House   26

Hessian soldiers   9, 12, 14
Howe, Admiral Richard   11

Howe, General Sir William   13–16
Howe, General Robert   22

Intolerable Acts of 1774   5

King's Mountain   24, 25

Lexington, Massachusetts   6
Long Island, Battle of   10

Marion, Francis   24
Monmouth Court House, Battle of   20
Morgan, General Daniel   25–26

Princeton, Battle of   12–13

Revere, Paul   6

Saratoga, New York   16, 18–19
Savannah, Georgia   22, 23
Southern Campaign   22–26
Steuben, Baron Friedrich von   20

Tarleton, Lieutenant Colonel Banastre   25–26
Treaty of Alliance   19
Treaty of Paris   28–29
Trenton, Battle of   12–13

Valley Forge   15, 20

Washington, General George   9–15, 20–21, 27

Yorktown, Battle of   27